T0103585

BOY

MAN

WORLD

MARTIN CHALLIS

BALBOA.
PRESS

A DIVISION OF HAY HOUSE

Copyright © 2015 Martin Challis.

All rights reserved. No part of this book may be used or reproduced by any means, graphic, electronic, or mechanical, including photocopying, recording, taping or by any information storage retrieval system without the written permission of the publisher except in the case of brief quotations embodied in critical articles and reviews.

Balboa Press books may be ordered through booksellers or by contacting:

Balboa Press
A Division of Hay House
1663 Liberty Drive
Bloomington, IN 47403
www.balboapress.com
1 (877) 407-4847

Because of the dynamic nature of the Internet, any web addresses or links contained in this book may have changed since publication and may no longer be valid. The views expressed in this work are solely those of the author and do not necessarily reflect the views of the publisher, and the publisher hereby disclaims any responsibility for them.

The author of this book does not dispense medical advice or prescribe the use of any technique as a form of treatment for physical, emotional, or medical problems without the advice of a physician, either directly or indirectly. The intent of the author is only to offer information of a general nature to help you in your quest for emotional and spiritual well-being. In the event you use any of the information in this book for yourself, which is your constitutional right, the author and the publisher assume no responsibility for your actions.

Any people depicted in stock imagery provided by Thinkstock are models, and such images are being used for illustrative purposes only.
Certain stock imagery © Thinkstock.

Print information available on the last page.

ISBN: 978-1-4525-2850-2 (sc)
ISBN: 978-1-4525-2851-9 (e)

Balboa Press rev. date: 06/15/2015

CONTENTS

BOY MAN WORLD.

The boy in the world will wonder
The man in the world will strive

The world in the boy to open
The world in the man to thrive

Boy Man World is a collection of poems, reflections and lyrics* written over the last two decades, with one or two from earlier days: they are offered here as observations, contemplations and anecdotes for you to enjoy.

During the mid 1990's I gratefully received a writing grant from Arts QLD with generous guidance and support at that time from Clare Hoey. The works to be written were intended for a compilation of pieces entitled 'Boy Man World', however due to collaborations with musicians Tye and Katie Noonan many of the works were repurposed as lyrics and the poetry book was not completed. Twenty years later and with a larger body of work to draw from I felt it was time to complete the intended work.

Perhaps these works reflect a journey, perhaps they point to a philosophy. I hope that in the least they tell a story that you can connect to and recognise. And so for the love and the good of all goes these poems.

With love
Martin

for the children

FOREWORD

These poems, this profound offering from Martin opens a space to experience a tenderness, a keen attention to moments of importance and an invitation to awake into deeper friendship with who I am beyond the surface - and to befriend Life as it flows without choosing the right or the wrong.

It swirls me in a good way to flow in this brook of insight that flows from a pure and bold heart.

I am so grateful for this kind of gifting - and welcome the possibility for more to come in service of a simpler and kinder world we all long for whether we know it or not . . .

Toke Moeller - CEO - Co founder of The Flow Game, The Art of Hosting and harvesting conversations and work that matters and the Warrior of the Heart dojo.

ACKNOWLEDGEMENTS

I gratefully acknowledge the love and support of my darling wife Jan and our children: Daniel, Nick, William, Sophie, Sam and James. Bryan for his wise guidance. Anthea for her inspiration and encouragement. Sam for his beautiful images. Will for his inspired design. Also to Shane Rowlands for her encouragement and direction in the selection and editing of the poems. Jeff for his inspirational friendship and brotherly love.

Alexandra Dolan - front cover illustration
William Challis - front cover design
Sam Challis - illustrations

I AM

I am dust and water traveling at the speed of life

Ancient father-mother
You who hold my song
And call me no name

Move an Om in your cavernous mouth
and between your teeth the fragile breath of my being

I am tentative as I bow, but not with fear
In the moment of supplication
your face is lost to me

OLD DUST AND TIN

In dust that walks
before the pale drive
of winter on Black Mountain.

Beyond cold spidering shadows
Cotter-River trees with-holding
their names.

In mist whispering
In the margins
of frost at Adaminiby.

Up under bogong
wings collected in the granite caves
at Brindabella.

I sense my dreaming.

And wild pig foraging down-wind
south south-east of Franklin.

The brumby kicking at
stars up on Scabby Mountain, where
rock was cradle.

Mallee root nubbed into the fire;
and the yarn over red-embers and billy-tea with
condensed milk sweeter than mother's.

And old Dido (grandpa's labourer since time)
wearing bib and brace
pressing down hard
on tea-softened arrow-root,
his gums and fingers
kneading the kind of tobacco that came in a tin.

THE TRELLIS

For Eddie and Jeana

We sometimes speak of the trellis,
where everything was cool in summer,
the house in the orchard; named Coolamatong,
"place of cool water".

To a six year old boy it was all adventure.

The passionfruit vines plump with purple promise.
The twin pecan trees, laying down their arsenal.
The hessian bag, for me to saddle the engine bonnet of a Massey Ferguson,
facing grandfather as he sweated through his silver moustache and straw hat.
The concrete water tank we named, "the swimming pool".
The dam at the bottom of the orchard: dark, cool and deep.
Big green frogs, skins glistening; calling and croaking at night.
And Grandmother Jeana's marmalade; full rinds and heavy syrup.

I loved the trellis. Covered in dense green Wisteria
branches as thick as your arm.
Its ancestry in the leaves,
in the firmament of twisting fingers
holding open tiny spaces for night and daytime starlight.

The trellis: a cool green blanket
under which we might comfortably spend the rest of our lives.
A place where I might wonder with grandparent's love
as we viewed the world through the same window.

A safety never repeated.

After my grandparents died, the orchard was sold,
we heard the new owners chopped it down.

When we speak of Coolamatong, we often mention the trellis.

Little Boy at Water Fountain

investigation of light shift
spanish inquisition to a button

stigmata of machinery
clear engine chrome

flow-mouth wonder
wild nozzle-play

fascination thirst learning tide
inch at a time

mouth of splash
rill
    river
        lip
           tongue
                eye-flash
silver

spooning the slurp-wet, when
fleet captain's patrol, cries, enough

squeals for more quenching

A FISH OUT

A fish out of water slaps
for the wet familiar
as first rainbow gasps
for all colour beneath
evergreen eucalypts

boy becomes hunter.

White flesh in the pan
rainbow now grey;
a dull eye pops in the fat.
The first meal of camp

"We're all about survival"
says the voice from the beard.

In that first howling night the tent holds no echo:
a cocoon of down
muffles the want of a scream
for mother's goodnight.

Terrain is now real, not just a geography lesson.

When morning arrives
relief and sunlight slap awake
the face of survival.
Mosquitoes frustrate zippered gauze, march-flies marshal to march.

Wisps of gum-smoke, the smell of the wild, steam from hot-streams on tussocks, beans in the pannikin, dust in the billy, tealeaves and gumtree chase the boil.

Longer walk today: boots even more ready for rubbing off skin.

Fourteen miles to the next creek and next water.
Ache in the pack
No rest only winter.
The dingo pads on.
Wild boar root en mass. Wombats rummage the banks.
Wallabies thump up the ridgeline.

"We'll circle our tent-line and raise tonight's fire after dark."
Says the beard and walks on.

The hunter
Seeks now no quarry
Dreams the snap of a soft sheet
and mouths words
for the water of home.

Saigon Battle Children 1972[*]

While I was learning to savour the new taste
of cashew and walnut in the autumn of that year
you were learning to eat the bones of your neighbours dog
as you fled from an earth gone moist
the leaves of war were torn from the jungle
as a cavalry of shrapnel burnt away the air
you were learning to hold your breath
while I was doing the same in a suburban swimming pool

when the dust of your family filled the lids of your eyes
being left to see for yourself held quite a different meaning
while your skin seared from the heat of warfire
I was feeling the warmth of a shopping centre in winter

when you went without feet,
a landmine exploding your underneath world underneath
I sprained an ankle at basketball
the words of an American god spat forth from an automatic weapon
and you saw the tongues of the lamb
inviting you to feast in a foreign language

and when I drew in crayon on the kindergarten wall
you were drawn in the crosshairs
just before the smell of cordite

MILK THE LIGHT

My father shouting at me
loud enough to wake my dead grandfather, the
red air is frightening I try not to tremble,
it makes him worse,
he hits me with a strap - but his anger soon passes.

Tonight the moon seems old,
if it cries it can cry for me because
my sadness is deeper than tears and
the old man I will one day be will remember this.

--

My mother, happy in her freedom swims naked in the bathroom
Swims an olympic record from the tap end
to the end where we keep the shampoo.

Beneath the waves she can't hear the
crashing and shouting from the next room.
The bathroom light is turned out,
the moon fills the bath with its soft-milk.

--

Sad is my sister crying tears like wet feathers.
Crying for a pain she wants to, but can't feel. Her tears
are starved birds that never learn to fly.

--

My sister cries the guilt of an expert,
My mother tends herself with soft lotions,
My father, a helpless bystander to his own rage,
wears spectacles passed down by his father.

--

Tonight the moon is my quilt
Heart-beats are held and all is muffled
The rage is the sea
My skin milks the light now.

INTRUDER NO LONGER

For Anthea

He sat by the river tree and
heard the whispering tale of trees
The great sheet of a cloudy day
hung above the river

The grey fish swam close
causing endless circles to ripple forever
A white ibis pointed its long neck to the grey sky
Unseen the fish sang singing the songs of fish

A white horse charged by
causing goat insects
to scurry into pink folds of skin

He sat by the Casuarina
Utterly hearing and seeing
An intruder no longer

An Invocation

The un-discovered country;
in his eyes
when he praises you.

He attempts to hide the nervousness
as the rate of his breathing increases.
His father never gave him praise. Never gave him glory.
Never it seems, made him the special centre of the moment.

And yet now he works this gift for you,
does so with no experience.
Is motivated by the desire to see you grow.
To see you swell with growing.
He stumbles over foreign land.

A son: your father.
Not measured by calibration.
Not perceived in weight or wonder but
as hard stone,
the slow carved mark
sharpening on
unborn generations.

You walk with him.
Your hand in his.
The path new, but well worn with wishing.

Father and son, two friends like fire,
like kindling, like warmth

If we imagine this for many sons and
for many fathers
perhaps
it will not be
so much further off.

Mother's Lullaby

With each year's Decemberness
The fledgling wills his wings to flight
Commissariat like he returns

He seeks again
A fondness kindled in the nape of mother's balm

Relieved respired
A mother sighs her lullaby
Whispering my son
My love
Comes home

THREE YACHTS

Three yachts scalpel the bay;
white tee-pees exploring
for an Indian Ocean.

Their wake, a healing incision
argues only a brief scar
on the afternoon tide.

Two children from Switzerland
playing with an Australian friend,
share the language of the shore,
count - uno, duo, tre; Italian
boats and moats in the sand.

I think of searching
the shape of my heart in another country

but today
the music of clouds,
the dialogue of quiet sun and sharing sea
is exploration enough.

AGE 10

Suitably respectful, and
never asking for trouble
or the time of day
I wait at home-station
like a cattle dog
My master, absent in the midst of a promise

My bones wait for flesh
My theatre
            for Godot

As factories burn
As droughts become floods
As Apollo is a god sending chariots to the moon

I'm ten years beyond birth already counting ways
to escape the infirmary

The hallway mirror
holds an apparition of silence
And over my shoulder
Is reflected a leafless tree
of seeming indifference

There may be leaves one day
but who can say

I wait
like Didi
for what I mean

THE BULLY

The teeth of hierarchy flash
a scowled curse in quick lightening.

This hard edge does not hunger for food.

His, is a stare into a desert battle-ground:
dry-rasping, gaunt and unforgiving,

A Goliath.
And me - envious of stones in the desert.
The 'Fuck you' in the eye of his razor.

My punishment waits like a
missionary's head in a bucket
(its smile still praising a tribal trophy necklace).

His armoured lips sip hot-dipped darkness
deep from the volcano.

The boy in class with my blood in his schoolbag.
The teacher dripping words of impatience onto my flight plan.

Head down, writing escape from the demon
Furiously - until the last bell.

A FIST GUTTING

Rodney the Tormentor
comes toward me, a slick sneer edging
the mug of his leering mouth
preparing the next barb garnished
with a delicate sliver of dry ice.

What's today's ridicule?

My hair too long, too short?
The art assignment a pathetic attempt at literature?
My bowling action; a cross between a mental patient and a broken wind-mill?
Knees too bulbous for any normal person?

Not today.

Like this, for almost two years
everyday
each day a new torture,
a new laceration of clean practiced words
and me accepting the torment with dull weariness
allowing the beast fresh meat.

I think, hope, pray, imagine
one day he'll stop
the relentless articulate brutality;
but he never does.

Not today.

The animal hunted turns
to find precision
and strength
in defiance
and then in all that follows.

Go,
now.

Rodney the Tormenter
goes down in a windless scream.

One blow
two years in the forging.

One blow
one strike
one out.

A fist gutting and nothing gets back up.

The art gallery attendant,
the other students on excursion
the teachers,
as if complicit in retribution
like a hypnotist's audience;
look the other way.

Rodney down
solar-plexus perplexed
and a new entry
in the part of Rodney's brain
that stores future possible outcomes
to hitherto unchecked actions.

Martin Challis

Decades later I can still see his face
in that ghastly micro-moment:
pain, shock, horror
and most surprisingly,
relief.

MAGIC DEATH

The boy who hangs his story from the bridge.
As if by fairy tale told minutely to a desperate lover.
Her tormented eyes
picturing this broken neck;
his story told in the lingering art of death. Or

he who faces the train to Ferny Hills
and each commuter who remembers
that day's monotony as bits of him
slapped against a carriage like
someone throwing wet fish. Or

the pass-over traffic
grumbling at the fall of tragic demonstration - a
boy not welcomed anywhere except by the earth
that took him in with a kiss of bitumen. Or

balanced on needle point, a
thousand thousand weights pressing death
into an arm embracing the TV-cable guide and
a torn photograph of Jennifer the mud wrestler.

And all this waste
sending little statistic waves of shock
that don't anymore.

Gone to sleep like the boys who left us.
Early sleep. Early rise and forget
the sons who disappear in a magician's finale. The cloak
of social history that accepts
this magic abracadabra
of disturbed unhappy youth.

A LETTER TO TELL YOU . . .

I think I'm pregnant to you.
I think our hearts have joined.

A poem is worth so much more in the delivery, so
I place my trust in Australia Post
and the efficacy of the clearly marked post code.

I heard that love is an intoxication:
so I purchased a bottle of wine grown in South Australia
and hoped to savour just a taste of you.

There's a chemical released in your brain when
you meet someone you love;
its dying to meet other chemicals.

However I can't cope with that kind of expectation
being too inexperienced for equanimous adjustment.
It's too much like needing a sedative from anticipating the sex you
almost had
when you thought your girlfriend was coming to stay for the night.

Don't think I'm bemoaning the fact that you're not coming to stay for
the night,
you live on the other side of the continent.
I accept the disparity of our geography.
I accept the arterial nature of the freeway system in human relationship
after all, its well known where all roads lead.

Did you know that if your name was translated in Spanish
I'd be interpreted as a conquistador with no hope in the tropics?
And did you know that I've always wanted to wear a superman suit and
keep nothing out but steady rainfall?
If you think about it, it's a potent philosophy.

Mephistopheles considered certain questions and theorems.
He found the intrusion of chaos theory and disruption to the order of
the work ethic unthinkable.
He found the mature and calculated response simple:
he told the bastards to articulate and pontificate elsewhere.
But please don't get any ideas.

This brings me back to my remaining piece of news:
Regardless of the fact that it's medically impossible
I think I'm pregnant to you.

Please write soon.

AFFILIATION

For Shaiya

On a dirt road
in affiliation and in the shade
my friend and I are speaking

We have our purpose
as do the trees,

tall trees
lisp and dapple in
conversant fraternity
and rubbing of shoulders.

We take one step at a time
through the conversation.

He laughs.
In his eyes wisdom pools for the dipping
if the thirst is recognised.

He advises me of inevitable disappointment that comes from expectation.

When the time comes for the aloneness of this contemplation
I cry into places empty of human ears,
into spaces too small to hide the fear of recognition
and think perhaps soon I'll be ready to carry the weight of things
and face the lion of my winterest thoughts who growls in the moan and
sprawl of me.

I put no promise into any thing,
weary with the longing for that which is impossible,
alone in the dream of a wished-for relationship,
the illusion of what could be tangible
the craving to be defined by another.

Later I tell my friend I wish to be set free,
to see myself as anything but a self.

And later still I find,
on a dirt road,
unexpected,

affiliation with the lisp and dapple of trees
and a thankfulness for the cool pad of each dusty step
that leads me on a road to somewhere other than disappointment.

IF YOU WERE HERE

If your mouth were a poem
a kiss would silence explanation

If your tongue were a bird
Song would never attempt flight

If your hair were laughter
Each curl would unseat apprehension

If you were here
I would tell you this

I would show you
why the heart
beats twice
with every pulse

DARK CITY

Black windows seen through night rain.
Wet as she waits for him. And the
low grey cloud as it sifts her barren sky kissing limbs;
she is the Dark City.

She waits. A she animal.
Soft cruel fingers prying for the rest of him.
Her hunger more insidious than his dependence.

A tender hand of pity grips like dark steel.
The crucible and chalice smelting one flame disturbed.
He burns in her emptiness. The half light of poison.
Eating at loneliness.

RASPBERRY TEA*

For Katie & Jamie

In the heat of the night
When everything is cool Is when
I miss her
The most

It was raspberry tea
No
Peppermint - I don't know

Lips wet longer when an afternoon
Came after
Noon
And went like clouds before clouds before . . .

You know
It is interesting to meet some . . .
Someone you can
You can
   You know
I don't know

We touched, like others
Like all others
Nothing new
Nothing new anymore
You want it so much
To be new
New for old is what they say

What do these old hands hold?
Old . . .
You want it so much
To hold
                It slips
You never did hold on very well
Its like   its like

I don't know, you want it so much

                I miss her

ADVICE FROM AND OLD FART

For Nick & James

Listen son
It's al 'right to feel
It's OK to cry
It's even acceptable not to be perfect
In everything you try

Failure can be a positive
If bent another way
A necessary back-burn before
The fire of success comes your way

Its not the end of everything, but the
Beginning of something new
It's probably the way you see it
Is the shape that comes to view

A mountain so enormous
Never seeming to be climbed
Until you've done some treading
Most likely one foot at a time

Some day you get right up there
You're laughing with the clouds
And at some stage you lose your grip again
Falling all the way back down

So you pick yourself right up
Spit gravel from your mouth
And head to other climates
I'm recommending south

On the way you meet a few kind souls
Perhaps a little wiser than yourself
Some who might begin to question
The state of your mental health

But don't despair; it's all good stuff
The journey, the quest, the sport,
Some days you'll go a long way
On others you'll pull up short

Just keep going that's the main thing,
I'm buggered if I know where, cause'
Eventually south goes north
And every other where

Keep treading, keep smiling,
Don't forget to breathe
It's important to enjoy yourself
And keep something up your sleeve

It isn't easy, this I know,
When some old bugger gives advice
You think he's a little crazy and
He don't talk so very nice

You're probably right, he might be mad,
But the thing about this is,
It's better to keep asking questions
Than be sitting in a tizz

Complain or question or kick or scratch
The ticket is the train you catch
The one for somewhere, the one that goes
Not sitting at the station and picking at your nose

Get on board
Live a life
Have some fun and
Cause a bit o' strife, now

I'm sorry I can't say more than this
But I reckon you know why; it's
Coz you've got a good long life to lead
And I'm about to die.

Reason for Poetry

when the sound of every car door slamming is yours
the ring in every telephone is you
when the whisper in every voice
the cast of every eye
the ball in every park
the call in every sonnet
the face in every smile
the bubble in every brook
is you,
          what is left for me to do
but write you down in every word
and read you,
over and over and over

SKYE

The loving stretch of your cloudy fingers,
your welcoming cob-web eyes.

How they haunt,
shake salt from the limb,
sweep up leaves in courtyards, and
carry their eclipse to the brink of me.

Tree's circumcised by gardener time
poke forks at you,
scrape your soft full plate
with the chafe of spidering knuckles.

Everything the flavour of sun-set is a plea.

What can I do when the wing of you
has nothing to say
but fall in reverse,

have you no pity,
you do nothing but sleep, yawn
and blink back your triumph.

Where are the places
I might squeeze you
into submission:
windows only take in so much.

Just once I'd have you secede at my feet,
break bread with the best of me;
release me from enthralled impatience.

I starve for some light conversation
but you practise your zen enchantment,
practise it right in front of me
day after day after day.

Show mercy.
        Crush me,
                do something.

I want you to fall.

A WORD TO HOLD THE SILENCE

If words were halved, such as gentle
men for example and used more often
in activities such as; policy debates, domestic feuds, jobapplications
and innercriticattacks, would more time exist for silence
and to the listening for it?

Earlier today I found a few minutes
filled with silence,
at that time my mind paused its chattering ways
and half of me was able to observe the other half.
It is something that I should like to do more often
as the experience offered respite from the
persistent need to be constantly explanatorial.

I notice this need often occurring in the form of an internal competition,
where two voices and sometimes more, vie one against the other
with selfcertified gladiatorial certainty.
One voice might say such a thing as:
'it is not good enough to rest upon your laurels – you must continue
to be loquacious and insightful, speak up and be cleverer'.
(Note the oftenused expression of 'you must', this is a favourite. Often
followed by: 'you should, they should and he or she should'.)

Another voice will counter; 'let him be, let him be simple, if he wants
to stop for a minute let him be'. This plaintiff voice however, will most
likely be overshadowed by another who will shout, calling me
to re-use words from my history, demanding that I repeat and rehash
them until I've succeeded in doubling and redoubling their meaning
into a meaningless re rehearsal of something that falls out
in the unresolved shape of complexity and disturbance.

The silence that I yearn for suggests to me
to continue halving words.
To play with them a while:
Thin king. Hat red. His story. Mind full. Am bit. Not ice.
And to continue to halve by half
with the half that observes the halving half.

I wonder will this help me to find just a word, just one
to hold the silence?

REST WITH ME

For Tim

The ebb and the ebb and the ebb of your sad heart dear friend. The
smooth wet weight of river stone; those sleek dark ears in their grey-
green window.

Clear-water sadness all the way to the bottom of the bed
where small grains furrow over the nose of an inquisitive predator.

I know so well your course and turn and how you stir
like an eddy above the tail of a hungry fish.

I see you rise and move. And swim
to another bend to curl into fronds that stroke you.

When you reach the surface, I fin-tickle your belly as
you stop the wing of a succulent dragon fly. I do not . . .

I do not want you to go just yet; to the drenching wilderness,
stay a while and bask in the shallows. Rest,

before you turn to the deep to hunt the elusive figment.
Stay a while and rest with me; empty your ears of whispering watery
ghosts.

CAMPING TRIP

Perfect with gravity
fuji-like mountain
above which hangs heaven
star full and bursting

beside which she sits with a mouth full of flattery
quipping alacrities with ease
'you're a man with a very smooth shirt', she says
'thank you', he replies almost inaudibly

The breeze brushes an inner thigh with its lycra tongue
she shimmers
as a clear-lake breeze kissed

He grows to become a campfire on her shores
she laps at his embers
reflecting and flickering

He encompasses the perimeter with stealth
Sniffs the wind for fear and for warning

none comes, so
they bathe naked ever watchful, for
a shift in the rushes, for the
fish in their sleep,
for the shadows
in the deep
not yet awakening.

COULD HAVE BEEN

He sees her in a gap through the crowd
She is a tall and boundless
beam of radiant light
a glance off the shoulder
more than and moving
away from flame
from neon
from whatever.

She places a fragrant perfume on the glass counter
of tomorrow's possessions
the thought is unbelievably sweet
but impossible to taste no matter how hard he tries.

He senses warning
ignores intuition
when inevitability smacks him
very sweetly in the mouth
brightening the day for a moment
but like a dying fingerling in a waterless stream
he grows dull and gapes for what could of been
but was never going to actually happen.

COLD TURKEY

I was
presumed missing on
an angry afternoons walk
across an ocean
of bitter pills
that swallowed themselves
in brown bottles
labeled caution
keep away from
me
and I feel
the scream of an angry after-blade scraping
across the glass that
keeps me
in this cell
you listening through
a telephone
grown surgically
from the hand
of providence
longevity
switching tables
when the waiter
wasn't looking
to eat the camembert
the cream
and all the opportunity
that was supposed to go around
like loaves and fishes
but I only see
an empty pond

and you floating
fat belly
full of everything
except the guts
to come clean
and to even give
a good goddam
but you don't
and now I'm out
and you will
'cause you're shitting
razor blades
and I understand
because
I would be to
if I were you
but
I'm not
don't say I am
don't ever say that
you know
that makes me feel good
when you're on the floor
like
the puss
I piss
saying
"fark man
I'm free
I'm out
I'm clean"
But no, no way
I'm all over you
forever,
I am so over you
I'm all through you
I am you
I'm the lane

in your vein
'freight train
to the brain'
I'm the reason
the mirror
barks back its bite
I am the only reason
you're out at night
I am you're only fucking reason,
don't forget it or
good night!

DROWN THE BLUE SKY

Drown in the blue sky
the blue sea
the green sea
and all the while, white waves, of wash,
cloud or mist arising,
on this rock I am every particle
I can see, and more than I am,
none of this, and separate is
my life a paradox continuum
inexplicably explained as
stable passing impermanence,
if I could drown in the blue sky
I would do it flying.

I AM HOME

the last of the sun's rays
linger through the stained-glass door

the latch-gate swings in the breeze
from the sea
stones to the hearth still warm
dust spots dance and swirl
in shafts of light

a timber venetian snaps lightly
against the window frame

familiar fragrances
console and enclose:
frangipani
freshly plucked coriander
cinnamon incense
a steaming glass
of ginger tea

the cool shaded hallway
pacific and obliging
reaches safely into every expectation

as a murmuring grandfather sea
continues to send soothing breezes

all the day's monuments fall away
peace is cool and still for a time

and I am home

APART

For Sam & Lisa

When you likened missing her
(in ways you didn't know you could)
to muscles aching after
exercise you hadn't done before

You said for you this was telling of a deeper love
And almost as if finding out for the first time
that love and pain are twins, you discovered
as a pair, that they, like both of you
are never far apart.

IN THE GATHERING BLOOD

On a back street in Mexico City meal sellers tend their stalls,
dark faced men feed from ceramic bowls,
menus are simple in black-board and chalk
everything is flavoured with chilli and
huddled shoulders reveal little small-talk.
Street lamps throw more shadow than light
and gas leaking from somewhere
feeds the air with an acrid scent.

I stop for a bowl of chilli-beans,
beside me and one over at the bar
a young man with matted hair and
heavy eyes unwraps a stained cloth,
takes a shard from a broken bottle and
neatly incises a small vein in his wrist.

He lets the blood drip evenly into a saucer
beside him and in the other hand holds what seems
to be a quill made from an eagle feather or some large winged bird.
Dipping the quill in the gathering blood he begins to write
in a leather bound book
on tawn-coloured hand made paper.

I watch every move. No-one seems
to care or notice that he does this.
He writes on and on, scratches a word,
dips again - the blood flows more slowly;
what has gathered seems sufficient,
he spits in the saucer takes a shot of clear liquid (probably tequilla) and
adds it to the mixture,
I assume this is to stop it coagulating.

My meal and appetite have gone cold watching this process.
When the blood-ink is all but used
he folds the book away, wraps his wrist in a stained cloth and
walks into the street of shadow and meal sellers steam.

The stall holder notices me and approaches:
"Si signor this is Miguel the poet of the people.
He is coming many times to write this way."
He smiles at me. I pay for the unfinished meal and he says,
"The poetry for the people is in his veins amigo,
is this not so in your country, are you also having such a poet?"

I leave him. Return to my hotel room.
Take out portable typewriter and clean white paper

And begin to write
in blood blacker than ink.

RETURNING TO SYLVIA

Returning to you sylvia in the black week of no moon:
the carapace
the awkwardness
aflame with evidence
the jew-net of Poland
-- your rack of guilt.

to fly at the sun or burn in its shadow
emptying pockets before you leave
you reap an abandoned harvest, but

the acolytes who call and call hear the ringing of rocks;
bells around the necks
of ghosts
lying down in
hallowed halls, somewhere bellowing

their words
    like yours
punishing me
punching me up the middle,
every image jagged remedy
my arse to my heart
jammed with grief,
throat swollen with loss

the case of your broken bits;
crockery splintered
in capsules or
shoeboxes or drawers carefully there, there

you are lips pressing
cold glass,
to kiss you to drink your warmth
impossible

after death I hear you;
crow sends your messages
but sweet sister that's not why you call

inimical oven: cavern and synagogue,
I am undone
discovering buried treasure.

in the breath of trees you are
somehow there,
in the quick-slip of feet across smooth linoleum
my mausaleum agrees with your arrival

but in the hour before dawn
in the silent roaring volume
you never hear of my love for you

we are cold lovers
both agony

SHE HIDES

She hides
In the edges of shade

She smiles
At an umber moon

She lives
Near the well at the bottom of my garden

I never see her

In the evening
I leave flowers for her

Some mornings
I see where she has kissed them

AXEL

Axel, who never had a rocking horse, once rode a bright blue tricycle.
He called it his 'Athenian Rhapsody'. He loved to play the tuba in bed,
and when he was feeling particularly happy, would sit on the loo in the outside shed,
pants around his ankles oompa-pa'ing till the cows came home.

That was quite a while ago; the tuba and the tricycle have gone,
yet he can still hear the triangle-sound the bell made on his tricycle,
and still remembers the scraping of the old keys on the ancient tuba.

Axel listens to old sounds very well (all the time):
he loves Bach, Mendelssohn and Donovan.
He loves to eat crumpets with honey and drink a large white mug of milky tea,
it reminds him of summer fishing trips to Lake Eucumbine,
mushrooms and gnats in the full-sun morning air,
(he loves to talk fishing when he's playing chess with Carl the orderly,
often quoting from his favourite magazine, 'Modern Fly Fishing').

Axel was once an expert at fly fishing; tying the 'super moonshadow' to perfection
(he named the fly after what he thought was a Donovan song, written by Cat Stevens).
When the hospital staff remember to buy him a new box,
Axel loves to drink Lady Grey tea made from tea bags,
he prefers tea bags, he feels that somehow they bring clearer definition to tea making.

Axel thinks a lot about definition,
noting how the edges of his bed are very clearly defined
by the clean-blue hospital blankets that drop suddenly
to the ocean of the grey linoleum floor. He likes the smell of cleanblue,
it's somehow a new sea to sail and sometimes the feel of his favourite
jumper
when he was a boy: a definite edge of beginning and end.
He knows that soon he'll cross the floor-grey ocean, sailing under a
white sheet.
But this is not a thing Axel dwells on for very long,
he prefers to think of such things as his next chess move
and flirting with Miriam the night nurse.

Axel has just beaten Carl in a game of chess. He's said goodnight to
Miriam,
a long quiet goodnight, a good long, good night.
He won't wake again, he senses this – and is peaceful.
When his last breath comes he hears;
a faint scraping sound and a single precious note from a triangle bell on
a bright blue tricycle.
They're good sounds. They are old sounds. They bring him . . .

NEW VACUUM

I put my lips to yours
We kiss away old skin.
Your face changes colour.
Becomes pink with new complexion. Then

your mother calls.
You can't tell her about this.
Instead you tell her ten, for coffee.

After coffee. At shopping. She remarks,
'my daughter is so very beautiful.'
The salesman nods in agreement.
She purchases a new appliance.
It matches the colour of everything:
the most powerful and efficient vacuum in the world.

She is happy. Brings it home. And plugs it into the socket.
It sucks up everything, including the pictures from the walls,
the curtains from the window and the telephone from its cradle.

Your mother is pleased; it's everything the salesman said it would be.
Along with the furnishings, it sucks both of us into its black belly.

Surrounded by the comforts of home we start a new life together.

One day you say, we'll be very happy.

But it's so dark I can't see your face.

The phone rings.

It's your mother.

She wants to know how we're settling in.

2:15 PM ROMA STREET SUNDAY AFTERNOON

the three of you
waving your brave little hands
smiling love and mischief at me
through the tinted glass
of the big green bus

I'm standing tight to the kerb
screaming at the concrete
as I smile
and wave back with gusto

'I love you'
mouthed in silence
'have I failed you?'
a silent question

I wave until you've turned the corner -
gone in a juggernaut like
stolen children

the street where we laughed
only a minute ago
now more empty than a new coffin

I walk back to the car knowing that we will go through this
again and again

every time you visit for the weekend

BLUE TO YOU

Blue to you may be a room with a view.
To me it's an ocean turned sideways.
It's the colour of air gone thick with the sea,
It's the largest and highest of highways.

Blue to you may be one without two,
And all of the times you've landed,
Feet thick with dew – stuck to each hue
Where you thought for a time you were stranded.

Blue to you may be a day that is new, to
Me it's the place where I'm standing.
It's the home of the eye and the reach of the tree.
It's the wave of the wind and the wave that is we.
Blue is the deep and the shallow the same,
It's just where I'll be when you're calling my name.

Searching and spreading. Dividing our wings.
Soaring the gentle, the sharing of things.
Come endless, come empty, full with your sound
call the vast harmony and arms that surround.

Come to the blue that touches all things
come with me gentle, come let us sing,
sing the high rising, sing the low mark
sing the blue heaven that covers the dark,
and chorus the carol, the carol of being,
and the blue that is given to those that are seeing.

IN THE JAZZY CAT CAFÉ

Domino's at their fingers,
the numbers
eating from the menu,
squares and rounds
enjoined but not sequential

In the Jazzy Cat Café
(tail curled in my mouth)

You weren't there
The sun had dried all the tomato's,
I was calling you unanswered
missing the rhythm of your character, and
the way you reached me with each impulsive smile
remembering earlier how . . .

we'd climbed eleven steps to your apartment,
and entered not really sure of where to next . . .

In another room;
(wooden floored)
was stored a blackboard menu,
a hostess offering welcome
in the way that sultans sometimes grin

I asked for panini without the mayo
the waiter iced the perrier
the singer sang without destination
which implied no journey

and I heard her song and
watched her lips
missing
  all the ways

that you might sing

INSANITY COMPLETED

complete insanity   and time ignoring the clock ticking   backwards
and forwards a child shunting a cart full of   blocks tumbling   down
a cliff   face at the window where I see a river running through   to
the end of year specials where christmas   cake always made with
old dough before baking should be let to   rise and fall of the
capitalist   approach to sand mining in Kakadu and lead poisoning
in tuna   fishing on the lake before breakfast slapping at mosquito's
exploited by greed overcoming the rest of us who are just as hungry
and   waiting at the table where i've waited for   days has nothing
to do   with me can we please take the attention off me   it's all i
ever   here and there is a way forward follow me this way   down
children in the deep dark woods lived a little dwarf with a pocket full of
thumbs cut from little boys who didn't keep their noses clean and out of
somebody   else's business to come here today and talk to you about
the theory of relative bullshit   which as you know was discovered by
Captain Jimmy the cook or Captain courageous Columbus or Hugo
weaving   its way into history before being   put out to pasture to grow
fat in a paddock full of Nowegian Wood   isn't it good that your father
is coming home after all these years i've waited   so long for the time
to wait   for a cup of tea would be very nice   thankyou very much
for coming ladies and   gentlemen please start your   engines of
the new age   old methods of brewing   handed down to you on a
platter and what do you do you throw it back in our faces   made of
broken glass shattered by the news crowds stand outside the palace for
days mourning the nations   lossst and found is this way sir broken feet
repaired daily broken hands twice daily broken hearts sir that's down
the hallway second door on the left in the cliche department sir thank
you sir your time has come i'm sorry it had to end this way   look i'm
sorry   enough of that sir   button up   there's a good chop to the
bottom of the neck   cuts air supply and results   instant lotteries are
the way to think of the   future is what you make of it   son before

you make any rash decisions   go and stand in the poet's corner and fill
in the forms you've been given make sure you answer every   question
is you must understand the rules of inquisition   without question
you must answer every question and make sure you complete every form
you've been   given make very sure that   every form is complete
insanity.

THREE MOONS FROM MONTO

Two friends circle the air
three moons from Monto;
friendship is measured in wingspan
in the joined eye of spiraling hunters.

Dusk before the day breaks,
loud cloud red
overlooks the dark steer
as it stamps its metallic breast
along the great snake's back;
its voice of tumbling rock
in a throat made for slaughter.

Hearing this and the language of insects
Peewees, Currawongs, Crows hop clear, but
the wedge-tail's majesty mistimes its ascent
and the impervious steer is unyielding.

Now one friend circles the field.

The dark steer moves on
hungry for interpreting silence.

Two moons reach into night
and for a third up near Monto.

ISNESS

Past and future mirror one another.
Fixed at their crossing point
Is an infinite and uncombustible present:
Isness as an endless ocean.

An ocean made of words
Fluid words endlessly mobile, where
Anything can be described
Anything foretold.

In deep and shallow utterances
Live all the metaphors
In cycling currents
All allusions ebb and flow.

Some tales are down for deep remembering
Some swim fertile yet unborn,
All the while the ocean shares her stories
Allegoric and relentless as they wash ashore.

SUMMER DAYS*

as you walk the path of plenty
as you sit beneath it's tree
as you sip on 'green grasshoppers'
that are good enough to eat
you chew the food of fancy
you eat the fatted calf
and those hands reach out to please you
expectations from the past

these are the feelings that you're feeling
these are the feelings of today
these are the feelings that you cling to
on high-hat windy summer days
these are the feelings that you hold to
as you struggle as you play

your pockets jingle full of coin
your wallet presses tight
will you spend your daily ration will you sleep alone tonight?
you are happy wearing chambre you are happy when you're paid
so you have a cappuccino and then work on getting laid

these are the feelings that you're feeling
these are the feelings of today
these are the feelings that you cling to
on high hat windy summer days
these are the feelings that you hold to
as you struggle as you play

you take what comes just as it comes and cling to nothing new
you might get sticky fingers and they may be tacky to
you can feel a faint reminder whacking backwards in your brain
you are living on a chessboard thinking warfare's just a game,
you are living in city full of people you don't know
yet you recognise their faces just enough to say hello

these are the feelings that you're feeling
these are the feelings of today
these are the feelings that you cling to
on high hat windy summer days
these are the feelings that you hold to
as you struggle as you play

COLD COMFORT

Rust, that un-used plough
vigilant in swallowing green
shares the fugue state
of various machinery.

And in tangible mist
milk-cans emptied flood the ground,
cows are sent back to pasture,
fence posts are made ready to burn,
in an afflicted winter
burning cold in the comfort of sorrow.

If an old crow happens at the cloudless
this is more omen
than the shrinking market.
And when the shoulders of my father
farming this winter
are no longer brave enough to carry
the sky
I carry his gun to the gate;
we walk a silent trail
to shoot the enemy
that never comes.

The cold sun is a bright nail
pinning us,
the blue weight
presses horizons from our reach.

My father
searches this expanse,
his hands extend
to something . . .
but I see
they only move
to wave away flies.

If there is any comfort . . .
my hand in his
is cold this winter.

SLEEP COMES

in bed - he lies awake
pleading
for sleep's, soft death
the laceration of each fragile memory
is a
knife sharp
thief
come to steal
thin peace.

in time,
desperate,
measured

sleep
comes:
his only suicide.

THE RIVER OF SHE

The hour hangs
a dark sheet unmaking.

Dawn is a moth, belittled in the first spit of candle-flame,
mandibles of first light slowly un-pinching.

The river of she will soon
leave on her own tide.

Warm in a homemade sea,
bed un-done
my sands, eyes, oceans, all one in the exquisite whirl
of ebb, flow and rise.

I seek meaning from the equivocal master, who teaches
cause of flame,
cause of sandal-wood, the soft escape
that unveils
the intimate distance of silent night and the voiceless sound of . . .
moth, bright with death.

And her last wish unheard, the river of she
Who passes through dawn

passes through the half-light of change.

FRIDAY AFTERNOON

the talk of heads
that all smile later
the fold of arms
the read news-paper

the bus stop
traffic, agitation
the driver late
the conflagration

a number plate
identified;
to run a red light;
to have even tried

the ticket stub
the validation
the tender fare
the invitation

the airbrushed smile
anticipation,
in magazine's
celebritisation

relationships that pass
through glances, two-
second flirtations
that take no chances

the nameless faceless
careless farewells
the hollow echo of
concrete stairwells

then finally
the doors we seek
to be safe behind
from week to week

KITCHEN SEDUCTION

To a friend who shares coffee
you offer sugar,
        love,
            and a biscuit.

Night trains, precise as a metronome:
the dark stranger lounging astride the kitchen window.

Emitting cool beacon, the
fridge-light undresses her briefly in the lick of its wake,
with sure signal.

Across smooth tiles
the pleasant stealth of bare-feet,
pad-soft and certain rapture:
seductive inclusion is
love like a biscuit half eaten.

CONVERGENCE

Crumbs of heaven
fall wing-soft
yet you and I
know nothing of manna or prophecy.

In the midst of
trodden
unbidden
inner indivisibles,
habit's anvils weight us.

Yet attest this to one small place of untouched bliss
where we may grace the light
now and so often
extinguished
in barren land.

The foreign treader
of a dawn held wish
unfurls from our robes,
hangs us at an altar,
and no-where attempts to keep secret the name of commitment
from the carol of each lip or tongue.

Silence the two-headed voice beyond the shroud,
hear this life
and the secret of light.

Entwine and wind
anticipate the
suspence and future of the imminent.

Hold off
hold off dear one
nurture such sweet convergence.

COLOURFUL BLAH

The vista
spiels with neon
Non-essential conversation repeats
Humanity hovers at the entrance
In this shopping centre every need seems urgent
Mouths pause their chatter
To sip at coffee or chow down burger
Gestures are reinforced with nail polish,
Jewelry on many fingers
small change passes across counter tops

In here the weather is neither warm nor cool
and everything designed to stimulate my mediocrity

Reflection in the shop-front is on sale at bargain price
but today I cannot afford to buy on impulse

I turn away to blend
With colourful blah

ENCIRCLE

I.

Awash
a broken spiral-shell
the stream of moonlight that spears the
imperfect aperture.
A delicate intention
the sure clutch of a seagull that turns this in the

foam of low tide
that weeps for a broken marriage. And
the sandy-wind turning out dried-up husks of baby turtles,
once clutched surely.

II.

A fisherman turns his head,
squinting from the moon to the sun.
Down through his nets are nests of old fish tales
and an old wife waiting for his return. Both,
ever awatch for the silver sprinkle under the wave-top, and for
a basket of fat herring,
thumped proudly on the table-top.

III.

A white-crane steps on a mirror behind the dune.
Fishes the land locked pocket with a spear in his beak.

An albatross,
no time for gulls or cranes and less for yearning nets, encircles.

The fisherman is for his pipe.
Fishing in his pocket for a pouch of backy.
And for waves.
And for wind.
And for silver.

EQUIPOISE

Neither this nor that
A perfect in-between

Spirit breath
Cosmic stance

The compression of a universe
Into one indivisible point

An expansion of a universe
into all points

A noun for oneness
Unanimous stillness

The experience
Of now

ESSENCE

you have given me the gift of love
abundant and imperishable
and with it I embrace the world
you have shown me love unshackled
cherishing every second of existence
a smiling love that warms the heart
linking friend with foe
burying all enmity and acrimony

governing and determining to brinks of passion
where sights unseen are revealed in glorious circumstance
your abundant love holds me high
and I walk strong in your praises
you have smiled in me, and
held me briefly in this perpetuity of millennia
you have removed soiled garments
and found a shining naked newness
I am bathed in the glory of your love
and am welcomed unto my saviours
guardian angels steer fate's course
and in celebrity hold cathedrals
full of chapels full of abundant joy

where bravery goes you are my courage
where subtlety lies you're my discretion
where strength is needed you are my sinew
where succour goes you are my comfort
where fate leads I will follow
you will always be the essence of my love

FAREWELL

Of chapel bells
and after day's dry summer wind
chimes angelic chorus
hangs in lasting configuration

My father's rye-grass covered hills
tremble with a breeze keeper's song
as he gathers up his grief

Mother folds away her weeping
folds away her dreams
until they are still

Mourners will soon move to chapel
They will offer compassion
and glances from a distance

My brother
born yesterday, took no breath
from summer's day

sang no breeze keeper's song,
felt no dry summer's wind,

yet heard
the farewell of bells
and dwelt there
harmonic
in tintinnabulation

FOLDING COLOUR

The colour of towels
hang in my house
down, like waterfall
from door-corners and window sills.

Some outside
some on wracks
All open mouthed
spread welcome.

I have paintings also. They are static.
The towels move around.
They're the colours of angels
blessing a clothesline
or bedroom floor.

If I'm wet they dry me
if they're wet I dry them
It's a good arrangement.

They smile at me, and often
break into laughter
when I attempt folding
they think it's a hoot
trying to fold away colour

FRIEND

I have kissed you in many mouths

I have tasted you
but not found you
you've been elsewhere
the curl of your tongue
forming a ribbon in wind

the cut of your hair
tied into shapes
I could make with my hands

your voice
breezes in phrases
I've reached for
their possible echo

I have waited to bend you
into my smile, how
my mouth has made its reasons
for wanting the shape
of your name

and the marriage of words
I have learnt
just to speak of you

I have called for you
devoured air for you
devoured my name
and not found you

are you there friend
now or waiting
or passing as a ribbon in wind
curling slowly
to the tip
of my tongue

FROM HIS WILDERNESS

For Jack

The way each hill runs down
The way tree-lines suspend the turbulence

My father's arms are in these hills
taking timber from the gully

The crest of his hat starts at the waterfall
his toes peep through lantana

His advice trickles into pools from the hollows;
as his boots peeled open, dry before the fire

Lizards bask like heat-curled nails in the sun,
billy smoke whispers its tale through the canopy

Through the slow step of a century
he has turned one-eyed squinting toward the sun

The scrape of sharpening-stone on an ancient scythe
sets my teeth on edge

The whistle to the bullock team calls me back
but it's too late, my ears have gathered for another harvest

I'm already removed from his wilderness

GRASS

Sedge
Rush
Cereal
Turf

Blade
network
Insect
canopy

Viral
fibre
Pattern
weaver

Earth
fabric
Meadow
aquifer

Wind
dancer
Tribal
mind

THE YOUNG CONCRETOR

His fixed black eyes,
turned, like a mother's to her sorrows
eight metres down in a hole
dug for concrete.

His workmates call hoarsely from the rim
but only see and hear
his nothingness

- "he was just here a second ago"

His neck is a broken spirit,
fingernails torn away, from
flaying the earth, falling infinitely
for one and half seconds.

The young concreter,
carefully finishing his glide work
at the edge of the slab
had stepped back to admire
the reflected perfection of the sky.

His mother receives the news before the slab
is no longer a mirror,
she pictures him falling and
thinks of the last time he called,

- "I spoke to him only yesterday"

FALLING

where cedar creek
falls
love of river rock
stands

my gaze follows
one wayward drop
sent further
by the breeze

the story
of this place
is told by clear water rill,
and the multitude of cicada
who chorus in the cacophony of daydreams

she sits
slightly away
I see the graceful bend of her back
the fall of her hair

and the delicate way
her feet
touch the water

HOMAGE

they call us in

the women
who bring us

through the eye,
the elder-wise mother
who is sister
daughter, lover, all

holding space apart
for us to enter

feminine shape
at the beginning

brightness resting in
and upon the earth

the tender choice

bringing light
to being

bringing cause

BRINK

an older man
clutching at straws
in difficult times
forgets himself the younger
when self belief
could walk on water
forgets the times, when
with water over his head
did not need to know
that straws existed

TEN COMMENDMENTS

One

The body is a song
Beat after beat the drummer keeping time
Saves one beat for you and one for the heart of the world

Two

When humans care for orphaned gorillas
They are human beings – being human
The gorillas
Witness to an endangered species.

Three

Three wise men arrive in Las Vegas. They're confused. The city of stars accepts their gifts in return for chips and exchanges their camels for Pontiacs.
Eventually the three men run out of goodwill and are asked to leave the star-city.
Now each of then wears self-correcting sunglasses, far more cautious when following the brightness of artificial light.

Four

The world is a box with clear sides
Through this we see the sky dark and the sky light
We see four directions on all horizons
And constellations that rise and fall
Shut your eyes and listen carefully
You can hear the lid open every time one of us enters
And one of us leaves.

Five

The lad in the schoolyard solves a problem with the same
Mathematical precision of his father
He counts on his five fingers and divides them
Into one tight fist
With this math he gets a perfect score and
None argue with the result.

Six

When all the world clocks stop ticking.
They will each tell of a different time: during rush hour, before the
interview, at the moment of martyrdom, just after take off, when war
is declared, the date and time of your birth.
On any given day each one will tell the truth - at least twice.

Seven

Seven sons were seven suns a'shine on everyday
Yet seven suns one day went dark to shine another way
Seven dwarves in darkening hue imminently benign
No longer to bright any sky and none would see the sign

Eight

Eight accounts of starving populations
Eight charity organisations seeking aid
Eight million raised per quarter
Quartered by eight reasons to extract a share
Before the rest is shared to the rest
Who continue to starve.

Nine

Nine millimetre cannon kills you with a slightly larger calibre than eight millimetre cannon. Makes a slightly larger hole, travels slightly quicker, has a slightly longer trajectory, provides a slightly louder thud or thwuk when it hits the target.
This knowledge may not prevent you from coming to harm; but at least if killed by nine millimetre cannon, you'll die well informed.

Ten

How many cynics does it take to change a light bulb?
As many as it takes to be satisfied with this as an ending.

THE GURU

For Michael

I have a friend who believes in cricket.
His belief is the belief of cricket.
His friends call him 'Guru'.
He can solve any problem for batsman or bowler.
However sometimes when he gives advice to a young player
his knowledge is rejected,
he accepts this with quizzical grace, not because his ego is hurt but
because to him, not listening to reason simply makes no sense at all.

'Guru' has greyish white hair and a slightly bent front tooth, he
usually wears some kind of goatee beard.
This gives him the appearance of something between a derelict and a
god.
His smile and candour have a way of keeping people warm.
When you get to know him you discover as well as cricketing genius
he is also a philosopher, poet and BMW motorcycle mechanic.

My friend is a most amazing man. He accepts all those
he meets, no matter how varied their opinions,
at the same time he pleasantly resists all those he meets
no matter how varied their opinions.
He is a great paradox.
Some people have greatness thrust upon them,
my friend thrusts his greatness upon people,
which can be amusing, entertaining and wonderful (for some).
He challenges peoples' beliefs, even their beliefs in cricket.
I love this man because he makes me test the structures of my own
beliefs.

My friend 'guru' has a very interesting pastime (almost a crusade);
he likes to convert the converters.
You've seen them: The Mormons, the Youth Ministry, the Seventh Day folk.
They come to his door. Some are repeat visitors bringing reinforcements
like barristers preparing a case.
I can see my friend 'guru' slowly converting all these people to the belief of cricket.
I suppose he believes that if they're going to believe in anything
it may as well be a subtle and entertaining art form.
That now pays very well at the top level by the way.
I picture those he's swayed in years to come playing in the green fields of heaven,
prominent white uniforms and broad rimmed hats,
field after field stretching out: the athletic constellations.

Perhaps the stars well lit limited-over night-matches that my friend Guru has recruited for the officer or guardian angel of the 'Heaven Eleven'.
This might explain his wisdom in solving questions of skill. I should advise Wisdens of this possibilty immediately.
Imagine if in this lifetime he is successful and
all the world's cults and religions and fanaticisms convert to the belief of cricket.
My friend would become very popular and widely respected
Perhaps even have his own TV chat show.
However what if he was worshipped and made a living god?
Then all the fuss would start up again just under a different banner.

Imagine genocide because of a bad LBW decision or ethnic cleansing of all left handed batsmen.

Or a cathedral built just for worshipping the ashes of leg spin bowlers. Popes and Bishops and Deacons exchanging their robes for umpires uniforms.

Possibly a world-wide class structure of administrators, umpires, commentators,

players, groundsmen, spectators and then at the bottom, sports critics. The third umpire watching everybody deciding if they should live (green)or die (red).

I wonder if my friend has thought his crusade through clearly.

He probably has, and knows that just like the people who won't take his advice

at cricket practice, even those he converts will convert themselves back to a belief other than cricket.

I should go and see him soon. I need some advice on my in-swinger.

HE COUNTS THE FISH AT HIS TOES

Weather's coming up soon lad, talk is, three days, no catch for a week then

Connors' folk slough to the Arms
in the shape of four or five,
a tawny pint floats the hour,
and by seven the place is alive.

My father now by the edge of the groyne
is a gaze half mast at the sea,
as he sails himself to the brink of an isle
and turns a yard-arm to the lee.

He sets on his oars the cataclysm of waves
he casts the wind at his hair,
swears salt is the sword in the taste of this life
and not what falls with a tear.

He'll treble a note in harmonica muse
and rustily suck a bone pipe,
spit saliva colder than frost on the grease
and never complain of the gripe.

Running the wind or roaring the cape
or rounding the sound of the wire
his name is the take of all seafarer kin;
the hearth, my heart and the fire.

My father the salt, the seafaring man
a wave in the seas as they glide
now found to the ocean,
a son to the sea
the son to the father; my guide.

HE WAS BIG ON TEA

A little empty that morning
she sat on the top step
of the verandah
sipping tea, sipping thought.
Three steps down to the pavement
squares of sandstone
lay in even handed rhythms;
flatly refusing to contour.

He'd moved away last week; big bloke, big smile
could clasp four pavers in one hand,
laid the lot inside ten days,
maybe a record, who could say.

Completed, the pavement was now empty of him,
no more scraping back, no more chipping out,
no more broad smiling hands
reaching for her cups of tea.

She missed this, as she missed the slightly flat renditions of
'midnight oil' and 'fleetwood mac', the cock of his straw hat
and the farewell call of . . . "see you sometime in the morning suze . . ."
(always at exactly 6.30 a.m.)

He was big on tea,
said he was glad
to meet someone who knew it
wasn't merely the dis-colouration of milk.
She'd smile at that, he was right,
things like tea were best, given time to infuse.
She sipped her tea, sipped her thoughts
and the deeper taste that came with a little time.

AWAY TO THE SILENCE

As the fire subsides
into furnacing embers
And the ocean's voice washes
in from across the field,
making ready for sleep
you offer a glass of peppermint tea
and wish for us a restful goodnight.

In evening's air, at night time's breath,
we sip and without word listen: to
crickets rhythmic and persistent as they
chorus out at the perimeter of shadows and stars,
to the gentle ones at rest on their perches
each with an eye on the moon
who call or croon at irregular intervals,
to the ageing house who creaks unevenly as she
shifts her shoulders from one
side of night to the other.

Then with a gentle kiss
and a last wish for good night
we turn to ebb
away to the silence
away to our sea
of sleep.

HOW LONG A STILLNESS

For Richard

sitting on the porch
our dog asleep at my feet
the sun leaves the longest shadow from the house

an afternoon is in the trees
they speak of a day of doing this and that
and acquiesce against one another's mischief

flavours of a garlic salad linger
salt-matted hair flutters against my forehead

the guitar rests
the book stays shut
the beer subsides to its last foam

a walk to the fridge for another
will happen sooner
or later

there is no telling how long a stillness will take

AFTER CUTTING TIMBER

at the top of the hill
I waited for you

not long enough for the magpie's
wing-feather to fall from the conifer

and then your silhouette
along with the sunset
struck me

and drawing closer
your smile

drawing closer

I LET YOU PASS

To my dead son or daughter
I left you
Let you pass
Kept you out

Frozen
The mark of
the palmist foretelling five children
I climb this hill now with four at my side

Your memory: A shadow on the distant range
where eucalyptus is to its last
the blue mountain

Though I climb and four grow
the wife that was then is now gone
her grief and her echo

Still I sense the soft pad of your call
the tug of your passing
and then almost
the first breath of greeting

I LOVE YOU

i love you i said
how is that she said
i just do i said
but why she said

why is the sky i said

why prove it she said
how can i i said
so you don't she said
yes i do i said

then why is the sky she said

it just is i said
that's what you say she said
just look at it i said
but it's not there she said

yes it is i said
then look up she said
so i did
she was right
it had gone
and when i looked back
so had she

In the Dream

The dream of death
where I surrender
is a fall to earth that completes me

on ground I learn
the last breath
will precede the first

and that when I have given names to all I fear
I will know these forms
and will call to my enemies

I will dance with them and embrace them
as worthy opponents

as teachers
who bring me fortune

I Watch Her Sleep

Morning
Soft light
And light sleeping

She sighs and lifts
sighs and falls

Her breath
the gentleness of day beginning

I sit and watch her
more lovingly
than a child could

ROYAL VISIT

We were sitting in the study in the wee hours
you on the couch
me leaning back in the office chair
our speech soft and humble.

I could see through the hall to the kitchen,
into view stepped the King of Rats
he halted when our eyes met
holding for some moments.

Snake-like, his tail wrapped several times around the room.
His regal gaze, considered me with no trace of fear
while mine was possibly one of surprise
and slight supplication.

Unhurried he stepped off
left the room and went on up the hall
- I did not follow.
You asked me who I'd seen
yet in yours eyes I saw you knew the answer.

Later, servant like - I cleaned the bench tops
and mopped the floor
Then gingerly set down a portion of food:
On his return - chambers would be ready.

With each sweep of the mop I could hear them building:
the rifle-crack of hardened wire
the snap of small bones breaking
the aftermath of silence

Sounds of uprising.

Sweet Man

For Dan

Some stars are set free to come live with us
Some live with sadness thinking they do not shine in this heaven

sweet man
you are not abandoned

you are formed in the shape
of brilliant light

you are brilliant life
in the visage of life

a free heart brother
cry not your river

your brothers steady you
in their rock arms

and in turn, you are
the expression of this

It is the Time

It is the time for love
Of course it is
What a thing to say
When is it not that time?

Perhaps it is never more
Never has been more
Than now
Yet somehow we wait
Wait for what?

Wait for higher authority?
When there is none to wait for
Wait for permission?
When it's there to give ourselves all along
Wait for someone else to go first?
When we are that someone.

Now more than ever
Is the time
For love, for
The telling
The giving
The living of it

A NIGHT-BIRD SINGS

What night-bird sings across the river?
What bear of winter whispers
low and deep in the cave of its mouth?
And who is she who moves toward the many mouthed artesian,
invisible to the clouds and stars that live in her reflection?

We stand on our heads;
the world turns its duplicity to meet us as
our imagination ventures beyond the beyond,
before it rushes back to be with she who has not yet released us.
She spins her arms in all directions;
our mother, calling with the night bird says
"here children you're safe with me".

We walk the southern bank of the Ballone.
Before the weir we imagine the river
mirror to all the world.
Then the weir-gates reveal her power.
Broken water announces our birth
and friendship;
a turbulent opportunity to bright with stars,
to carefully wake the sleeping bear.

Beside this river
Our future is brought together,
And like her, this unseen strength
Will flow potent, low and deep
and with our mother
nurturing.

Just Now

When you are where you are
Just there
Not elsewhere
Not spinning
Or toppling
But steady
Ever steady
In the breath of being
You are
Just now my darling
A universe at its centre
A wondrous
Infinite now

LIVING FOR SUCCESSFULNESS

In this room at four a.m. where the universe sometimes meets, I cram some thinking time into the stillness that does not occur at any other part of the day. A wall-clock scratchily taps its one-tone metronome in a time signature disquieting to most industrious thinkers.

This contemplation is possessed with a version of unkindness that has arisen out of unsteady dreams. In the most recent frame: *invading forces stay out of sight to threaten as the unknown enemy. We burn candles for those who plead the safety of our dwelling. But suspicion becomes our ally and neighbours are offered no solace.*

I notice a small moth as it circles a candle avidly craving for the feast of light. I think of those who have struggled with a near-death experience. I'm told the dying enter a beautiful light when called to begin passage from this world to the next. Does the small moth feel a sense of wonder as it prepares to feed the candle?

The lifeless screens of television and computer, (sometimes channeling the universe into this quiet room) hold their square black mouths agape, but offer nothing more than mute obedience. The only living pixel in this room is worshipped by the fervent wing of a moth: and is unaware of being defined as metaphor.

I hear at distance, the first bus for the morning passing by, it is mostly empty of the silent ones it will carry later in the day. I wonder how many of today's travellers will have been awake at this time, pondering fate and future in the shelter of an urban meditation.

The early hours of the morning, I'm told, are when most passengers depart for the next world as they sip or gasp a last breath.

Slipping by and above me, some adventurous souls are carried by a hot-air balloon: the rushing light and sound of the gas-flame is a jet of life which heats and sustains the commercial moon as it drifts by in close orbit. The balloon then morphs its metaphor and mimics sunrise.

Perhaps moth and balloon and empty screens are pre-cursors for all that is to come today: all that is furtive, all that is futile, all that feigns omniscience, all that is agape, all that is sufficient for those of us who assume we will live on and on and on. And for those of us who repeat each day secure, content and satisfied: completely taken by all the fuss and noise of living for successfulness.

FRIENDSHIPS IN MANY FACES

Fiion

a beach ball floated on the waves
it bobbed and rolled and went along
if i was fishing that day i would have seen it
- there on the beach
and above
a hang glider left the grassy cliff
to swing his feet in time with
sea gulls who never tired of laughing,
he saw their white wings and the crests of the waves beneath him,
they were one and they were many
but there was only one beach ball
floating and bobbing along. laughing
in many colours
at the fish in their sea
and the birds who looked like clouds

Ant

a happy face floats in the air
it has a curling ribbon tied to it
i think it is a balloon
yes it is
a bright red balloon

Eli

crystal jar - tight sealed lid
full - full as you can be
bursting sometimes with colourful buttons
of all sizes
they are names, and when you call them
they dance
like fireflies scattering into dark places
they light the world with campfires
we are warm, apprehension runs away when you
sow these buttons and
we're all well clothed
with garments so richly fastened

Cassim

a feather brushes the nose
of the giant
will he sneeze
or carry the bird?

Kit

excellent tennis is rare
I think of Wimbledon
the best of the best
the court divided
as are the spectators
they cheer, they sit in silence
they see you serve, they see you lob
they see you backhand a winner
they see the choice of the chosen
and when victorious
you accept the trophy
and the defeated

Kit - again

ok you're a bird
fly
fly above the nets
don't stop for trees that
look like antennas
and when you pick through leaves on
the forest floor and
find the king of worms,
eat him slowly
he will feed you forever

Shem

the sharp sword cuts sweetly
it works with cool incision
knowledge is apprehended and
the red well flows over
fields are rich
strength knocking timbers
builds a house,
we live and eat well,
your house prospers
you are graceful
your love is light
and good air is for inhaling

LEAF GATHERER

She takes autumn down in fallen leaves
Sets some on glass and some in pages
Wraps others in fine tissue.

She gathers the fallen hands before each winter
Along remembered pathways
On afternoons once stepped in adoration.

Before snow lines the sparrow's nest,
Before silhouettes make empty the brocade of winter's edge,
Before the grinding teeth of winter's rock.

She clasps these hands together.
Holds their colour tight
to all the light that can find them.

She cannot forget the confetti of shedding leaves
their colour and the sun in burnished reds and auburns.
The garden pond they strolled by, the leaf-strewn grass they embraced
by:

Or the grove of a September proposal on the avenue he left by
and the promise to return that falls each year:
with all the leaves of autumn.

NAKED ON RIVER ROCK

The smooth force of virgin skin
caresses and moulds me in stone.
I stretch to the contour
groin the hollow
nurtured and naked
for sacrifice.

Grave friend, grey faced
steady eyed friend
shallow edge
great heart
melt with heaviness the torsion
in each of these limbs.

I surrender time to the mother of you,
dry tenderer, assauger of guilt, you
who holds up day, who lets down night,
who bundles and sprawls me
like a rough shouldered parent.

I search for the place of no light in you,
close my eyes to your dreaming
seek out eons you've sloughed off
and deeper, how your weight pulls the gravity out of me,

I surrender
and can fall no more into the rocking
rocking lap of you;

mother how can I fold into you
how can I surrender
how can I add my breath to the sigh of you?

MUSIC IN THE MAGIC*

music in the magic in the mystery
of softness in the footsteps
that your voice takes
to the place within my heart

brings a secret fascination
for intrigue's imagination
where enchantment chords a yearning
willing obstacles to part

yet when music is discordant
or when sadness floods in tides
the fear is overpowering
for the little boy who hides

but with childish laughter promising
the joy of trusting smiles
I wonder for the soft heart
set free from all denials

I wonder for all joy of things
as they bubble as they soar
I wonder for the song of love
on the path of evermore

music in the magic in the mystery
of softness in the footsteps
that your voice takes
to the place within my heart

AFFAIR

Lie in the bare-faced sun
savour time
under seige
frittering hours
afor breakfast and

rush 'round
later
if necessary
under fire
moving appointments
while telephones twitch,

anticipation

then forage
the howl
create havoc
hunt the giggling
play for keeps

afor heads
roll apart
        In an ultimate shudder

MY WOMAN

My woman is a guitar.
She lies next to me.

When she is playing
I like to be a song on her lips, however
They are made of steel and
My fingers hurt if I play too much.
My woman is the guitar on my bed.
She is my best friend.
When we cry together we cry the same tune.
She is a good listener and I am also very attentive
I caress her neck pressing carefully near the backbone,
she is always grateful.
I love the way she smiles with an O shaped mouth.
Sometimes at night when we are making love
cats and possums hear us through the bedroom window
They go crazy
they think it's a circus.

MY COMPANION

For Pamela

True love is my companion
She guides me in delight
She whispers all the names for love
With soft attending might

True love is my companion
A swirling heart of one
A blaze of pure intention
An illuminating sun

True love is my companion
She dreams beyond my dreams
She is where the compass points
And all that's in between

She is sunlight bathing
A soothing gentle breeze
Water from the mountain
Harmony and ease

True love is my companion
As gentle as the dove
Within the heart's dominion
My companion true, is love

NOT LEAVING

I'm waiting for you to leave me
but you don't

I'm waiting
for perspective
to re-appear

for
diminishing return

for warmth
from distant
appreciation

but you don't leave

I'm inhabited
the meal doesn't end
the wine re-fills itself

surely time will take you from me
a little further off
so I can wave
the small wave, of

loving friend

rather this
than retain the air
    where you might have been

imagining that you hold me

as you do

OLD JURIEL

poppies in september,
remember Juriel?
and seedlings

he came walking up the garden path
puffing grandpa smoke,
wrens jumping

the garden tap, dripping time drops
into the bird bath,
we ate crumbs

after autumn
the tennis stopped;
too cold to pick onions

tea cake in the sun room,
Juriel would laugh
gold teeth chattering

willow banks and cricket,
off to join the Luftwaffe,
before the season's over

the thermos always leaked
and the tattered wicker basket,
we kept them anyway

excellent hydrangeas
second prize, open division;
however, the pomegranate marmalade disappointed

the cliff that day,
seagull squadron on standby,
Juriel saw only the blue

noiseless it was
marmalade got on everything
gold teeth scattered everywhere

MORTALITY

You fly high
in the night
seeing nothing below
or above
but the absence
and abundance
of light

Ancient wing;
stroke of genius,
deliberate cruelty,
you preen each red feather,

particular to the
last breath
before flight

OLYMPIC COLOUR

there were painter's clouds that day;
broiled and tumbled,
moving inner purpose across an easel.

beneath them
a concrete mind mixed and etched
one long brush-stroke;
the tarmac before us.

excited engines carried us along
and carried by us
an air befriended . . .

with the convertible top thrown down
your hair streamed behind
olympic colour; a spectrum of extraordinary.

your head held back a sunrise laugh
and all the wind
belonged to exhilaration.

The horizon captured another sky,
a mist-green hail filled sea; that ominous litany.

A pallet knife scratched its lightening
and the danger of no potential
that kept us moving on.

OUR POEM

for my darling

I woke at 2.30am and left you sighing gently as you slept,
checked the trap but found only droppings on the floor
I set the trap again and hoped the rats would leave –
I would prefer not to kill anything.

The dog mawed and moaned at its fleas
rubbing against the rail on the back verandah,
it settled when I whished it back inside to sit
(my mouth made that wist noise, the one you know the dog will hear
but won't wake the sleeping).

I lay on the red couch in the study and read Ray Carver.
A return to Carver simplifying me. If not by sleep I was
comforted by his weave of innocence and knowledge.
Ray started writing poetry in the year I was born (1957),
I don't know why I mention this, perhaps I feel him like a kindred
spirit and am warmed by even the slightest connection.

Between the living and the dead are the sleeping. However being at rest
is no excuse for ignorance. Ray is at rest - some 18 years.
His poems like me are alive and breathing.

The magpies begin their morning carol as I return to bed at dawn.
Your breath and skin have waited for me.
When we wake, I tell you,
I am grateful our poem continues.

AS ONE

Within and beyond
your self
is another
self

And other selves
within and beyond again

Within and beyond
your self
are all selves

All beyond
and within
as one

RAINBOW

Tucked under and lifting a symphony of cloud
The sun beams in lay-lines from its horizon.
Yet, the scientist who explains this phenomenon
Cannot describe my feelings for such a spectacle
Cannot describe the song in me that dances
The miracle of light and spectrum.

—

You are mighty, you are ethereal
Your many fingers rake aberrant their spatulas of light
Your beauty makes all else ghastly or at least ordinary.
The trifles of each day's turnings are insignificant in comparison.
A conscience of orb, mist, shadow, light
The Gods derive pleasure from your presence
Else their thunderous growls bemoan your magnificence.

—

There is no darkness just the absence of light
There is no cold just the absence of heat
There is no disbelief just the absence of your benediction.

Uncapturable, delicate, infamous portent
implausible ultimate spectrum:
Your house is where I worship

CONCORD WITH ANGELS*

For Bill

On the thin narrow track of a stare into time
A lonely soul treads a single fine line
Razor edge cleft, pit fall either side
Through echoes in chasms where emptiness hides

The tread of the dead, the beat of a drum
Sounds of a symphony as this new day comes
Return of the fallen return of the saints
Homecoming of brethren through life's timeless gates

Through portals of promise, quickening and skies
As clemency lightens as majesty flies
Released and unburdened no flesh can deprive
Unbound and unlocked relinquish all ties

Now rest in epiphany thoughtless and soothed
Aware and reflective, harboured in truth
Now rest and replete, sanctuary unfold
In concord with angels life's love to behold

LOVE HIM

Reach toward him
the little one
there in your hurts and fears
Look toward him, not away

You take your soldier to war
guardian at the perimeter
with the ark-light of blamelessness
yet you leave him unattended and he is bereft

Look toward him
the little one
locked beneath the carapace
hidden from your tender heart

You are discourteous in attack
blind to empathy
Righteous in argument and thesis
yet none are healed or reassured

Look inward soldier
to the little one
his fear has become your fear

The child within is not yet comforted

ON THIS SHORE

My friend Sonja from Serbia
taught me to pole-fish
with a string of moonlight
by the lake
beyond the tree line
where stones
at our feet
grew wet.

On Sundays we'd trade
with fishes
for loaves
and plenty
from old-man Sheady.

On that shore there were no comparisons
for lovers in Kosovo;
where lakes were not known to keep their fisherman.

Now you and I stroll by this sweet water
and cast a few stones,

we sink a leaf or two
as each trajectory defines our harbour.

Our children believe
It is their parents who make this shore safe:

beneath a harvesting sun
only the scare crow is ominous.

SAT AND LISTENED

On the 4th of September
I returned to an empty house,
a wall of anger ran through me and around me
It took a week for that wall to crumble,
standing at the cash register at work
anguish surging up from a deep well way down low.
For hours I sobbed and howled
in the office out back of the store
Evelyn the manager came and went
and when she could – just sat and listened.

Three days later my mother and father arrived
for two weeks they stayed
their child, the grown man needed care
mother cleaned all the shelves and cupboards
cleaned all the clothes and ironed all the shirts
father tried to find the answers
and in the end – just sat and listened.

After they went home, the house slowly lost their comfort,
shelves and cupboards returned to slight disorder and
one by one ironed shirts were worn, never again to feel the same.
Hanging in its place I left one shirt untouched,
now and again I would open the wardrobe
to feel my mother in the sleeve.

A decade later we are speaking on the phone
about the children
all of them young men now and mostly independent
you talk about wanting to see them more often
and it being hard to arrange, you tell me about your new man
and how things are working out.

In a moment of candour you speak of the past
confessing
it should probably never have happened.
Who would have thought that in the end
it would be me, who just sat and listened.

SHADOW MUSIC

I am a craftsman. My hands are made of clay.
They're soft and wet and mould silhouette.
The last I made were without shadow,
The next will be more musical.
They will be spin around me -
Chimes in a western wind. Chimes of a different figuring
perhaps to hang in branches, simply as decoration.

If I rest, there will be no forming.
I fear this.
I fear the unmaking and forever sleep.
The chimes will awaken me with their shadow-music.

****

Squalls and storm clouds move inside me.
I hear thunder. Some say
they see change coming.
I see constant weather. There
is purpose in their forecast,
no in-decision and in a precise moment
the exact snap of thin ice.

****

I awaken before a bridge - reaching far across a rocky canyon.
Going to the edge and leaning over I see
the darkness of endless sleep. I hope to hear
water song and the expanse of rain-dreaming.
I wait at the bridge for a traveller like me to pass -
I will ask him to describe his journey and
The way ahead, which I have not yet seen.

THE ANSWER

For Toke

The sought answer
The endless search
The elusive entity upon which the holder of knowledge wishes to triumph
as a theist reaching epiphany.

This beast in all of us
hungering for
answers to questions the natural world never seeks to ask.

In seeking the meaning of things
in seeking the meaning of meaning.
This endless relentless pursuit
to capture an ultimate metaphor
upon which somehow everything might turn,
and somehow be possessed and understood.

And then within all the pontificating
The blunt fact slaps:
there can be no return
to the cocoon
to the cradle
to the womb
to re-curl magically into unknowing pre-form.

And eventually the wisdom to see
and perhaps only after exhaustion,
in the nothing more for it,
in the I've got nothing left, of it,
to cease an unskillful pursuit

And quite simply to find
it is simply wise
To live longer
In the space beyond explanation
In the body and the being
of the question.

THE GENTLENESS OF CONTEMPLATION

With the first awareness of morning
I sense the kind of clarity elusive
at other times of day.

She is a singular breath, formless,
offering insight into the endlessness
of something pure.

Yet she moves away as thoughts come:
those dissenting armies that tramp in
to involve me in the containment of opposites.

She will not be held in place by argument.

I long for her when she leaves.

My intention is to attend to her when I'm able.
To be the gardener who loves the flower.

That she might touch me when she will
That she might find me, often

In the gentleness of contemplation.

GREY CRY

Wet winter on a beach
everything is grey

sky and wet sand

decorates the feet
of seagulls
skylarking
hauling left-rights through the gusts

Seaweeds embellish the foam
Bobbing their heads
up now and again for rescue

Each rush of wind seals an escape from
sense and
silence

In the maelstrom
I merge into obscurity
The sounds of my weakness unclear

Smooth nothing
black and white
paradox

not dangerous
not visible
not cloud mist or tears

THE EXPERIENCE

Whatever experience you are having
Know that, it too shall pass.

Know that at times it will be okay to be not okay
And that, this too shall pass.

Within every experience
something will be there for you.

It will either touch the truth of who you are
Or it will ask you to look closer to find that truth.

On looking, the truth of who you are will draw closer
With patience, with acceptance, with courage, with love, with practice,
you will touch it but not hold it.

Whatever experience you are having,
It too shall pass.

THE WILD MAN

For David

I love the wild man,
He is generous
His sun-glint splits its beam
from the eye of energy
and sparks any dull kindling
to high awakenings

he will come chanting at storms
he will rave in ecstasy
annihilating the heavy dread
that holds the comfort bound
who hover already wrapped
awaiting uninteresting death

my medicine is to dress in his war paint
to love the wild man
to love his love of life
and let him take me to the abandoned places
wild that await within

THERE IS WORK TO DO

In human history
For the centuries
that can be remembered
Perhaps the most destructive force
That has lived among us
Is the human mind
That does not observe itself
Is human thought
That is unaware

MORNING WALK

For Chris & Jane

Walking down the hill
I think about the view

Walking up the hill
I think about the hill

THINGS BRIGHTLY WRAPPED

gentle rain soothes our rooftops,
clean cool waves
pleating into corrugation

rivulets remind the grass to grow,
worms, to inch along
toward warmer heaven
and grass to yearn for soft feet

we know we'll determine
things by this
we'll say
the softer words that come from water fall,
we'll hold up lanterns for a homecoming
take up letter writing
and be diligent in all we see
through windows,
rhyming couplets and things brightly wrapped,

hold frangipani in its fragrance
and tropical night in avocado air,
and fall, just like rain,
if we can;
with nothing more to do . . .
nothing more than letting go

Martin Challis

THIS SYMMETRY

For Jeff

To see where you're coming from
To get you
To take you seriously
To understand your deepest intent
To legitimise your ways of being
To love you for you
with no conditions

This symmetry of friendship
to balance worlds

To the Regiment

Night's armaments
tethered by a lone street light
wait as a patient carnivore
watchful and certain

A cigarette glows
in one man's mouth
as others blow fog, puff into their hands
shuffling to and fro - they're shipping out tonight

Arguing up the hill
a truck in the middle distance
comes to take them to the rally point

Whistling in this town
will be left to young fresh faced boys
when they think on their fathers
the soldiers

Tenements in formation stare unblinking
each window an eye transfixed
Rubbish bins, curbside, at attention, seem to anticipate
instruction or disturbance

Martin Challis

A gathering mist pads the rooftops
as the townsmen heave aboard,
with one last glance - slightly checked
each man searches for the loved ones
who are
silent,
asleep
or at prayer

THE ROAD TO RETALIATION

child-small voices sag
bomb-smoke rises from the ground
far off, birds still shake

Billy Striker blown
to Holland, the north sea wind
took weeks to fall

beforemourn chimneys
slate rooves yawn hunger,
one cigarette draws breath

moon crater on the
road to Derry, limousine
sarcophagus lands

siren scream and scrape
tears rigor mortis frozen;
the sea now quiet

hands across water
missing fingers, Gabriel
silent, the watcher

he'd stopped to look
smile asking the time of day,
pressing the trigger

one small death for man
one giant death for mankind,
eyes search behind moons

bicycle wheel turns
awkward lazy arm protrudes
broken flaying skin

obliteration,
scalpel dissects argument
camera's detail

a.m. paper print
fortresses build stone by verse
each wall a chapter

retaliation,
leopard stalking, counter plot
begun in blueprint

burnt flesh of kingdoms
republic's frost bitten dogs
bark anger blood sex

interrogation,
splattered kneecap agreement
hands shaking silence

investigation,
no stone unmoved, evidence
a silent quarry

old man keeping dust
one eye swollen, hunching armour
his grief in buckets

TOGETHER

For all our conversations
It's the silences I remember
Quiet times
In rooms together

You attentive to the preparation of a letter
an essay
or considering carefully,
music you're about to play

And me sitting on the sofa
Reading Carver or Whitman
Quietly appreciating your contemplation
Pretending only to be interested in what I'm reading

I do not tell you that your presence completes me
Or
How you feel from across the room

I do not say,
I am grateful for your company

KIND TEACHER

When crippled by the fear
Of what others may think

The kind teacher speaks these words:

Your power lies within you.
Life endowed you eons ago.
Your work today is to know this deeply.
Your power does not lie in the minds of others,
you do not need their approval for what you already posses.
As you practice today keep your attention on giving,
on being generous without the conditionality
of it being reciprocated.
In this moment now and in this breath you are free.

No Explanation Needed

I look over my shoulder
you're watching me,
with a green tree-frog sitting on your shoulder.
You're both smiling.
So am I.
Your photograph goes on repeating its smile, day after day,
it never tires
or has a day off,
just waits to share a bit more of your enthusiasm.

You're there as I wake each morning
reminding me we're inseparable.
Even now I can hear you say,
"you know the river finds its way,
you know the tree was once a seed . . ."

Two thousand kilometres, separate cities, separate lives
serve the paradox of our closeness.

Your photograph reminds me
love will reveal itself with each day.
The 'I that loves you'
is beyond us both,
to understand it
is as impossible
as interpreting the smile of frogs or the speech of trees.

'I love you'
lives outside a definition;
there's simply no explanation needed
as we inhale.

SLEEP AS METAPHOR

when there is nothing left
but the need for sleep
all the body can do
is close the eyes
it will not need
for a time
and find the hollowest
part of a calming memory
to tuck away into
releasing the need
to hold anything
save the desire
for peaceful
slumber

from deepest rest
there can be a return
to the world where
possibility re-awakens
and with morning
the opportunity to
go again
to attempt what had
the night before
been unimaginable
and unknowable

Martin Challis

Loss Makes Us Grateful

at first learning
grief brings the un-returnable message
there is no un-reading
no un-learning
only unbearable immutable fact

in solitude there is no escape
in connection there is no solution

over time the seven stages are traversed
and while there can be no forgetting
with acquiescence
there can be acceptance
and with it
a gentle light of loss
illuminating
deepest gratitude

OF CYNICISM

the voice of cynicism
with imperious wisdom
informed by circumstances past
where through defeated expectation, corrupted naivety
perhaps wounded vulnerability has been
disappointed on innumerable occasions

and chanting incessantly
in a cavernous register
"there is no hope – there is no point"
and louder
"there is no hope – there is no point"
and louder still
"there is no hope – there is no point"

would have us adopt this epigram as our own
in the belief
that if we do
the prophecy of self determined hopelessness
will be validated and affirmed

its unspoken fear of course is that we will leave it there
abandoned and alone in the cavern of its own arrogant despair

so here's an idea
surprise it
take it with you
out of the pit
take it for a bicycle ride on the beach at low tide
hump it in a ruck-sack up a rocky ridge
swim with it in a lake with a sandy bottom and willow banks
invite it to the funniest Robin Williams film you can think of
above all else, let it experience your unconditional positive regard

constantly
continuously
repeatedly

offering counsel
in all the tones and voices
of unrelenting love

HUMILITY

I would like to know you
More than I do

You are a gracious presence that in glimpses
I have seen influence the mightiest egos acquiesce

Somehow at times I stumble across you
yet would know you more as a constant companion

I forget you often and in the throes of reaction and defensiveness
catch myself in arrogance or in self righteousness or justification

Which is always followed by regret

How do I know you?
How do I find you in the moments when I am alone and embattled?
How do I find you in that first breath?
Of surrender

What is Natural

For Jan

As a breath
will happen by itself

As water will find
the way to flow

As gravity will hold
us to the ground

I will love you always
and this will be
as natural

AFTER RAIN

Cedar Creek
a moonlit evening
looking up
into sparkling eucalypts

After rain
The moon is reflected
In every droplet
On every leaf,
Simplicity has sent her messengers

With the brush and rustle of an evening breeze
These celestial missives begin to fall

To leave
the moon more eminent

DEATH

the unequivocal
sentinel
a living metaphor
arising
from the gesture
of simply

letting go

A COMPLETE AND JOYFUL GLIMPSE

for Sophie and for Ollie

inspecting momentarily
the visiting sulphur-crested cockatoos
leave our pine-tree for another, further down the hill

en masse, they fly towards and just above us,
their screeches, loud and unmistakable
are full of enthusiasm and committment

some, slightly smaller in size, are silent
I wonder if they're the understudies of the chorus
closely following flight-lines of their elder's character and bravado

these beautiful creatures, so independently defined
raise a cacophony that exhilarates
every fibre of the soul and fills the heart with laughter

self-less, expanding and enraptured
I briefly lift to the massing of their flight:
a complete and joyful glimpse, of full participation

FLIGHT

For Anthea & Ivor

They have a ball here,
their backwardsing
their forwardsing;
the rainbow lorikeet, the pink galah, the dove.

Along and up and down
the ridge line of this hill
like an airway
a real high-way upon which they fly;
the joyful chattering squawks and squits
of sheer intent,
to move
quickly to the next excitement:
a blossom, a floral, a pod
a nectar.

And then again to
dash about,
to go together
and all this urgent
all this such essential fun.

SOMETHING RETURNED

All of us, all of us, all of us
trying to save
our immortal souls, some ways
seemingly more round-
about and mysterious
than others.
We're having
a good time here. But hope
all will be revealed soon.
from Ray Carver 'In Switzerland'

something has returned
there is poetry again

my son James has a shower;
the rose drips ratter tat on the bath
as if in pantomime
for James
who loves to drum

I read Ray Carver
and find it possible to love some one I've never met

in a fathers arms
I weep and tell him I'm afraid to let go

tell him
life seems one long obligation
tell him

there is no poetry without water fall

APOLLO BAY*

(Co-written with Dan)

Wont you come on down to Apollo bay
You can take the coast road all the way
In the morning you will see the sunrise
A shimmering birth
Spilling orange from the sky

Come see the herald's dash there gold against the grey
Won't you come on down to swim it up via Apollo bay

Come see the flashes of the schools of hunting fish
Won't you let me tell you about the joy of all of this

Surge beneath the cauldron of the cliff's amazing size
Roll beneath the waves
As they boil in the morning light

Wont you come on up via Apollo bay
You can take the coast road all the way

Wont you come on down to Apollo bay
You can take the coast road all the way
In the morning you will see the sunrise
A shimmering birth
Spilling orange from the sky

A LESSON ON DROUGHT

for charles c frost

. . . we couldn't help thinking about our
experience in Canberra years ago

as humans are wont to do, we looked to
the sky for signs of rain
but day after day there wasn't a cloud in the sky

what we failed to notice at the time was that the birds -- those
gorgeous rosellas, the grass parrots, the cockatoos, and the "silly" gallas
-- were going about their business unperturbed
in God's good time
the rains came, of course

and since then we've seen photos of snow on the
hills about the city; a rare event, we understand . . .

with age, with time
we do understand
much more now
we remember the dear ones
who've passed by
like cloud-shadow slipping quietly
from the circling hills

old dear friends are nearer to us
and we are
nourished upon their reflection

TAKE IT ALL

take rain from sky
take the way tall men straighten your stance
take the students of dance
see the little ballerina stretch her toes
see her mother warm with the floodlight

take your plea to the judiciary
take your eye to the statue of David
smear on the dust of Somalia
rub raw the frost of Croatia
refresh your aim in the heights of Angola
but do not stop only at this

take every impediment
trust every promise of clemency
stumble if you will
fall under cease-fire
take it all

take the watchmaker
bent over time
with fine tools
clasp each second

take the sculptor who
chisels and scalpels for the grandiose

later in your armchair
fold creases in your newspaper with care

Martin Challis

with every nourishment
with the cloth of your nakedness
make sail for your harbour of origin

remember the milk of your mother
warm or cold or sweet if it is so
appease hunger
with the ambidextrous mouth
of a soldier
fed with death in his jungle

be the bystander, the bi-partisan,
the cripple, the timeless,
the dancer
be it all

take each increment
the infinite
and fundamental present
take it all

COMMON GROUND

For Peter

On common ground
We weed our differences one by one

We plant the you and the I
In a circle of friendship

We meet the soil with outstretched hands
And as we grow together

The significance of what we do
Becomes un-utterable

MORNING REVERIE

For Anna

Between grey sheeted sky, and
grass green covered fields

Among dips and contours
clear rain water pools

Magpie and Currawong
engage the other in carol and furtive call, in

Clear precise statements, morning reverie,
tuneful trill and soulful segue, their

Full repertoire of robust conversation
brings song, community and particular joy.

ACROSS FIELDS

For Pamela & Anna

Wind patterns
Wide the grass plains

Fans dance invisible
Her caterpillars

Cloud shadow
Racing their backs

THE DISPROVERS

"In a spiral galaxy, the ratio of dark-to-light matter is about a factor of ten. That's probably a good number for the ratio of our ignorance-to-knowledge. We're out of kindergarten, but only in about third grade."

Vera Rubin

In questioning existence
It's purpose and
Our place in the universe
The disprover looks for evidence from the Galaxy.
No matter how extraordinary the measurements
Such as the size of the sun and it's distance from the earth
The ratio of dark to light matter
The number of atoms in each molecule of carbon
The countless number of solar systems
The disprovers find no evidence of purpose or cause.

I wonder if they
might be looking
In the wrong place?

THIS IS NOT A POEM

crash the barriers
test the waters
ask the curious question
make a list of to-do's
include
- put the weapon down:
abuse
glock
razor
fire-cage
gelignite:
whatever
just put them down - if not
how should you proceed?
terror rises in the east
fear rises in the west
does each
respond in kind?
curious word, kind
no kindness in retaliation,
do solutions exist?
crash the barriers
test the waters
grieve the stricken
forgive the horror
whatever ways you decide
remember
this is not a poem.

ON THIS NIGHT

For Kerry

At the end of our road
A straight road
Of dusty gravel
Well trodden in all
Our passing
The waning eyelid moon
Rises omnisciently, anointing
a bedazzled sea;
light-scape dappling, dancing.

On this night
at rest at sleep, like
many others, we may
not attend
the ancient eye, in
perpetual orbit
slowly winking
her way to shut.

PLACE OF LEADING

For Gretel

Who will lead us when we do not lead ourselves?
Who will know us when we do not know ourselves?
Who will love us when we do not love ourselves?
Who will trust us when we do not trust ourselves?

None.

When we name what gets in our way of leading.
We find the courage to speak what is true.

When we name what gets in our way of knowing.
We find the wisdom to shape our world.

When we name what gets in our way of loving.
We find the heart open to find the heart.

When we name what gets in our way of trusting.
We find the will to move beyond fear.

We find our place of leading
And others know this
And find it
through us

BEFORE THE BEACH

Along the swale
turned upside
down behind the windy-windy
there, capturing a moment
as keepsake
before – just before the foredune
crests in green belted
spinifexes and tail-back blooms
the salty sea shakes away
and forefront washings tide the shiny sand flat
as we marvel gambol frolic free;
liminal at the margins

WHERE LIVES SUCH HEART?

For Cobber & Gram

Great heart lives
In the sea of dreams, where
The gentle soul knows
The wonder and power
Of even the smallest ripple, and to
Touch just one
With love's caress
As testament profound
To life well lived.

ALL OF US

For Toke, Monica & Jan

coming in by the side road
a winding path
to the stream
took us down where
we sat for a while
feet bathing in cool water
attending the natural theatre
so many quavers and characters in
the movement of rill and brook,
ceaselessly purposeful, over
stone, sand and moss

this going around, under, through
us, here we gather, and have gathered for millennia
we are the ancient flow
from first mothers first fathers first family
the tribe are near
coming out of the ages we
hear their call and chatter,
in time we come to know
this all of us, our story

RED LAND

For Douglas

In a land well trod
not flat but deep,
etched in lines of song
on ridges red by ochre
and once upon a time, by slaughter.

This at the hands of our fathers.
Now hidden in history's shadow
the ancient's heritage not well understood
or anguish felt for them, whose suffering
echoes across seven generations.

What could be cherished
with such spirits - the gentle natured wisdom
that does when recognised
nourish and unblemish
the white wash of ignorance
that once invoked atrocity as necessity.

To pause and touch this capacity
for recognition, to offer meagre apology
as but a humble first limp, albeit powerful beginning,
to ongoing actions of forgiveness and compassion to
heal this red land and join in unison
the lines of ancient song.

BREATH OF GRACE*

For Shane

The eye at the door looks back at the room
Where I sit with my pen to complete,
The standing the falling the settled are set,
The words that come quickly I keep

They release a brave two-beat, strident and true
To portray in a metre stepped out
As an uninspired word or excessive verb
Flakes down to the dust at my feet

The rhythm that comes the image that flies
Bring patterns I wish to embrace
Like flocks that will dart or schools that will glide
Or herds that will run with the beast

With passages lain, new shapes array
To foretell or observe or describe
Emotion may grow, inspiration bestow
As a stream from steep mountain's reside

The writing that heals as an unction reveals
All the magic of words in a line
As colours are painted and craving is sated
To know the words I've just written aren't mine

END GAME

extrapolate retaliation
to

age of suffering

end game

nil
all

IN TRUTH

If by fear
I am contracted

It is only the gentle wing
of forgiveness
in courage
and love
upon which,

I can again expand

TO SEE

the illusion of ego
is to believe that
my reaction, my trigger
is your fault

TO WAKE

(Harvested from Art of Hosting)

The enemy
My friend
Wakes me up
And I am grateful

THE CENTRE

At the centre

Of your being

Is a mystery

Quieter, stronger

More silent that imagined

You can anchor there

In all seas and seasons

It is close by,

And always possible to

Enter in simplicity

Such stillness

THE SIMPLICITY

Wake up
to the simplicity, to
essential stillness
the natural breath
the calmest force
weaving
weaving
dancing

skilfully
delightfully
at the heart
of the heart
of all

Where to Look

Turn my head
To what is simplest

My heart
To what is true

My body to
It's deep knowing

Each sense
Each pulse
Each rhythm

Intuition anchoring
elemental truth.

HOLD THE STARS

For Will

As children we learn to hold the stars in sparklers
Orbit them in all directions to
Describe our moons

One day we realise they're far away
We place an eye at the end of a telescope
And search for memory of simpler days

BIO

Martin lives in Northern NSW with his wife Jan. They have six wonderful flourishing adult children between them. He is a poet, an actor, a teacher, a facilitator and personal and executive coach. Martin has a deep love of the natural world and a life long passion for learning.